MAKE it WORK!

MAPS

Andrew Haslam

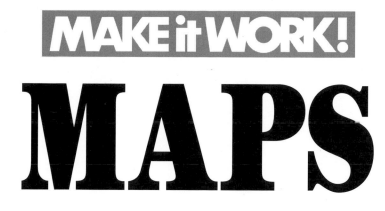

Consultant: Steve Watts, FRGS

WORLD BOOK / TWO-CAN

First published in the United States by
World Book Inc.
525 W. Monroe
20th Floor
Chicago
IL USA 60661
in association with Two-Can Publishing Ltd.

Copyright © Two-Can Publishing Ltd, 1996
Series concept and original design © Andrew Haslam

**For information on other World Book products,
call 1-800-255-1750, x 2238.**

ISBN: 0-7166-1754-4 (pbk.)
ISBN: 0-7166-1753-6 (hbk.)
LC: 96-60461

Printed in Hong Kong

1 2 3 4 5 6 7 8 9 10 99 98 97 96

Text: Barbara Taylor
Editor: Robert Sved
Art Director: Carole Orbell
Senior Designer: Gareth Dobson
Additional Design: Helen McDonagh
Senior Managing Editor: Christine Morley
Managing Editor: Kate Graham
Production: Joya Bart-Plange
Photography: John Englefield
Picture Research: Lyndsey Price
Model-makers: Melanie Williams, Peter Griffiths

Photographic credits:
British Library/Bridgeman: p28(b); British Library: p10(tr), p29(tl); British Museum: p28(tl);
Dr Eckart Pott/Bruce Coleman: p13(tc); Greenland National Museum & Archives: p4(tr), p28(tr);
NRSC Airphoto Group: p40(t); Oxford Cartographers: p38(tr); CNES, 1994 Distribution Spot Image/Science Photo Library: p45(tr), p21(tr);
ESA/PLI/Science Photo Library: p22(t); Tom Van Sant/Geosphere Project, Santa Monica/Science Photo Library: p5(t), p6(t);
US Geological Survey/Science Photo Library: p45(br); JP Delobelle/Still Pictures: p13(tl); Zefa: p32(tl).

Maps:
p4 © Quarto Publishing, © Zermatt Landeskarte der Schweiz, © Geocart, © Crown 85069M/Ordnance Survey,
© Crown/Courtesy HMSO; p20 © Slovenska Kartografia, © Crown 85069M/Ordnance Survey;
p25 © Instituto Geografico Nacional; p27 © Arno Peters/Oxford Cartographers; p40 © Universal Press Pty Ltd;
p41 © Teito Rapid Transit Authority, © Universal Press Pty Ltd; p43 © Crown 85069M/Ordnance Survey;
p44 © American Express Publishing Corporation Inc.

Every effort has been made to acknowledge correctly and contact the source
and/or copyright holder of each picture, and Two-Can Publishing apologises for any
unintentional errors or omissions which will be corrected in future editions of this book.

Contents

Being a mapmaker

Geography helps us to understand what happened to the Earth in the past, how it is changing now, and what might happen to it in the future. To try to make sense of our world, people make maps, pictures of the land, to record and share information about the world we live in. Many ancient maps were based more on stories than on facts, but today's geographers have a wealth of information, gathered from **satellite** pictures and computers, to help them to describe our world.

Why are maps useful?
People first made maps to help find their way across unknown lands or seas, or to record what land belonged to them. Explorers drew maps to record features of the lands they visited. People still use maps to find their way around, but today's maps can also tell us about people—where they live and shop, and how they farm the land.

△ Not all maps are flat. This Inuit coastal map is carved from wood.

▽ People make maps of towns, mountains, and even stars in the sky.

Types of maps
You can show almost anything on a map, from weather forecasts to animals of the world. Maps showing natural features of the Earth, such as rivers and rocks, are called **physical maps**. Maps showing how people use the land for farming, transport, homes and so on, are called **human maps**. Some maps are general reference maps; they show a variety of features, such as landscapes, forests, towns and roads.

A historical record
When someone draws a map, they use the information available to them at that time. Old maps tell us a lot about what people knew of the world in the past, and the ideas they thought were important. Looking at old maps, we can see that people did not know as much about the Earth as we do today. Some mapmakers of the past left out large parts of the world from their maps. They filled the gaps with pictures of monsters or clouds, because they did not know what was really there.

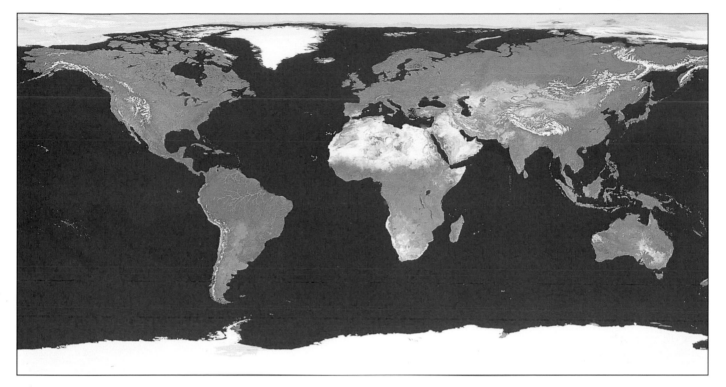

Using this book
Geographers have to study a wide range of subjects. Throughout this book, we have used **symbols** to show where information relates to particular geographical topics. The symbols are:

physical   mapmaking, or **cartography**

weather   route-finding

human   **global**

Make it Work!
The Make it Work! way of looking at geography is to carry out experiments and make things that help you understand how geography shapes the world in which we live. Just by studying the models and reading the step-by-step instructions, you will be able to see how maps work.

Safety
You may need to use sharp tools for some of the experiments in the book. Ask an adult to help you. Some of the activities take place outdoors. Be careful near rivers, lakes, ponds, steep slopes, cliffs and busy roads.

△ *This amazing picture is made up of many different pictures taken by satellites out in space. You can see clearly many important features on the Earth's surface, such as the white tops of mountains and green areas of forests.*

◁ *Satellites circle the Earth recording information for mapmakers.*

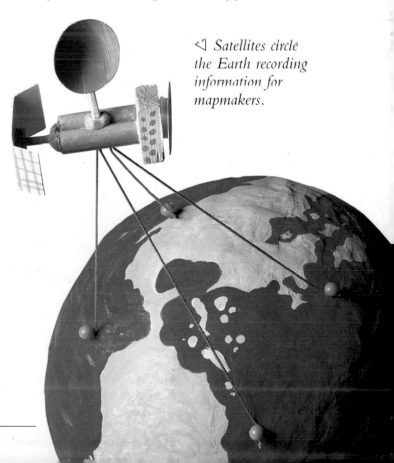

A bird's-eye view

A map is a picture that usually shows things from above, like a bird looking down from the sky. These days, airplanes take pictures from the sky to help people make maps of the land. But maps show many things besides what you see from the air, such as hills and rivers. Weather forecasters may use the outlines of the land to make weather maps. Architects often draw **plans** of the inside of a building, imagining how it will look from above.

Satellite photography

Satellites hundreds of miles out in space can send back images of the Earth showing amazing detail—sometimes down to areas as small as 100 square feet. Some satellites can "see" groups of trees, or even individual large trees. Satellite images are especially important for mapping places such as mountains or **rain forests**, where it is difficult for people to gather information on the ground.

△ *You can see the branching pattern of the Amazon River on this satellite image of South America.*

▷ *These models show how the view of a valley from a helicopter changes, as the helicopter rises above it.*

1 View from the ground
Imagine you are going for a ride in a helicopter over a river **valley**. Before you take off, you can see how high hills and trees are, but it is difficult to see how far apart they are.

2 Oblique views
As the helicopter rises, you can see the valley from a slight angle above the ground. This is called an oblique view and it helps geographers understand the shapes and positions of features.

looking down

1 Lay some objects on a low table. Look at the objects from the side and draw them. Now stand on a chair and draw them from above.

2 Look at how the shapes change. In which picture is it easier to see the positions of the objects?

✏ Layers on a map

Maps of places can give us a lot more information than photographs. Although they are usually flat, maps can tell us about the height of the land, show us what buildings are used for, and even reveal what is under the ground. Lines, colors and symbols are used to stand for the different layers of information.

✏ Drawing plans

Detailed maps of small areas are often called plans. These are used by people such as architects or builders. Architects draw pictures or plans of what they want a building to look like. Builders use these plans as a guide to tell them exactly where to put the rooms and how a building should look when it is finished.

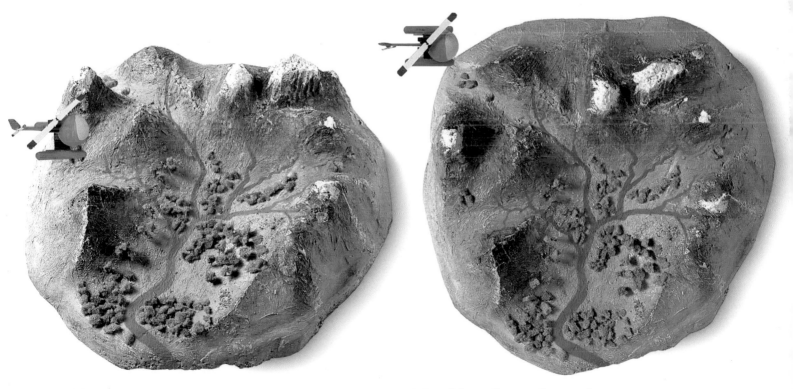

3 Rising up

As you move farther above the valley, everything looks flatter and it's not as easy to see where the land goes up and down. The trees appear to be flat green shapes.

4 Looking down from above

It is now easy to see how far apart the different features are, how they connect with one another, and how to move between points. This is why a map showing a bird's-eye view is so useful.

Scale and grids

On most maps of the landscape you will find two important pieces of information: a **scale** and a **grid**. A scale is something that tells you the actual size of what is on the map. A grid is a network of horizontal and vertical lines drawn over a map. It helps you find places and describe where they are.

✦ Reading grids

Grid lines divide a map into equal squares. Each line or row of squares is labeled along the edges of the map with letters or numbers, so people can describe any point on the map easily. These labels are called grid references. To work out a grid reference, you usually read the labels across the top or bottom first, and then those along the side. This pinpoints a particular square.

△ *On this landscape model you can find certain features, such as the mountain in grid square 0203. The lines cross at the bottom left corner of the square.*

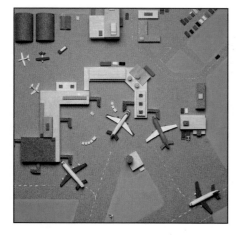

1:10,000 or 0 — 150 — 300 feet

1:6,000 or 0 — 90 — 180 feet

1:2,000 or 0 — 30 — 60 feet

△ *As the scales of these pictures get larger, the view of the airport gets more detailed.*

✦ Scales on maps

A map that is drawn to scale is the same shape as the landscape it shows, but a different size (nearly always much smaller). The scale tells us how the map size compares to the real size of the landscape. For instance, four inches on a map may represent four feet, or even four miles, on a real landscape.

✦ How to write a scale

The scale can be shown on a map in two ways, as shown above. It can be written in figures, such as 1:50,000. This means that one unit on the map stands for 50,000 units on the ground. Another way of writing a scale is to use a bar divided into units. All the units represent the same distance. This is called a linear scale.

DRAW TO SCALE

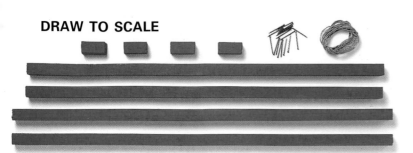

You will need wood strips, thread, nails, glue, hammer, tape, saw, paints, paintbrush, small objects

1 Using a saw, cut two 16 in. wood strips and two $16\frac{1}{2}$ in. wood strips for the frame. For the legs, cut four short strips. Paint the pieces and leave them to dry.

2 Glue the frame together, as shown at right. Hammer nails into the joints to make them stronger.

3 Tape lengths of thread across the frame every 2 in. to make a grid as shown above right. Now add numbers or letters to two edges of the frame.

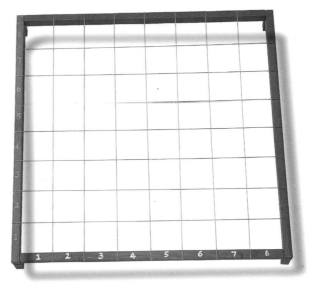

4 Place some objects under your frame. Draw an 8 x 8 in. square on a piece of paper and divide it into a grid—like your frame but smaller.

5 Looking at the objects from above, draw what you see in each square onto the equivalent square on the paper. Because the side of the grid on your paper is half the length of the frame, your drawing has a scale of 1:2.

Getting larger or smaller

Small-scale maps show large areas with little detail. A map of the world, for example, is a very small-scale map. On large-scale maps, such as town plans and road maps, small areas are shown in more detail and features appear larger.

△ *This is a 1:2 scale picture of the objects. This means that all distances on the drawing are half the length of those on the real objects.*

Measuring height

Maps of the landscape need to show the height of the ground, and mark any hills, valleys, coasts or cliffs. Information about the height and slope of the land is useful to drivers, hikers and cyclists, as well as to builders or engineers planning roads or railways. **Three-dimensional** maps can show clearly how the land goes up and down. Flat maps use **contours**, shading or colors to show height. Hundreds of years ago, mapmakers drew little pictures of hills on their maps, but these were not very accurate.

△ On this 18th-century map of part of southeast China, the mapmaker has shown height by painting the hills and using colors to show different heights.

⛰ Contours

Contours are lines joining places of the same height. If the contours are close together, then the slope is steep. If they are widely spaced, it means the slope is more gentle. If there are hardly any contours, the area is almost flat. So contours show both the height of the land and the shape of the slopes.

◁ The lines on this landscape show places that are the same height, like contours on a map.

MAKE CONTOURS

You will need acrylic paint, plasticine, colored string, toothpick, thick wooden board, glue, cardboard

1 Build a plasticine landscape on the wooden board. Decorate with acrylic paint. Place the landscape in the tank.

2 On some card, mark lines ³/₄ in. apart. Glue it to the side of the tank. Pour water up to the lowest mark and scrape a line with a toothpick on the landscape to mark the water level.

3 Pour water up to the next mark and scrape the next contour in the same way. Repeat until the landscape is completely covered by water.

4 Remove your contoured landscape from the tank. Now highlight the contours by pushing colored string into the grooves, as shown above.

△ View the contours from above to see how they would look on a map.

△ Mountains and hills like those above can easily be recognized on a map. They are represented by rings of contours inside one another.

spot height (in yards)

33   45

△ A cliff is shown by contours ending suddenly. The cliff face is marked using black lines called **hachures**.

🏔 Shading and colors

There are other ways of showing height on maps. Sometimes shading is used. This shows the shadows cast by hills, as if a strong light were shining from a corner of the map. Colors are also used to show height. High ground is usually colored purple or white, and low ground is yellow or green. This method is often used on maps of a large area, such as a whole **continent**.

🏔 Spot heights

Some maps also include **spot heights**. These show the height of the land above sea level at certain points on the map. Spot heights are often shown without any contour lines. These points are only marked on the map and do not exist on the ground like **bench marks**. Bench marks on buildings or posts show the height of a point on the ground above sea level.

Signs and symbols

Symbols are the language of maps. They are simple signs that show what and where things are. Symbols are used on maps because there is not enough room to draw pictures of everything on the map. A lot of information can then be presented in a small space. Symbols mark physical features as well as human features. For instance, a blue line may represent a river and a black square may be a railroad station.

Landscape symbols

On maps of the landscape, symbols are used to stand for physical features, such as woods, rivers, marshes, cliffs, beaches and hills. Hills are often shown as brown contour lines. Marshland may be indicated by small spiky tufts of grass. In a woodland, it is not possible to show every tree, but mapmakers usually have symbols for the two main kinds of tree, deciduous and coniferous. Deciduous trees lose their leaves in autumn, while coniferous trees keep their leaves all year round.

▽ *See how the physical features of this landscape model are shown on the map opposite.*

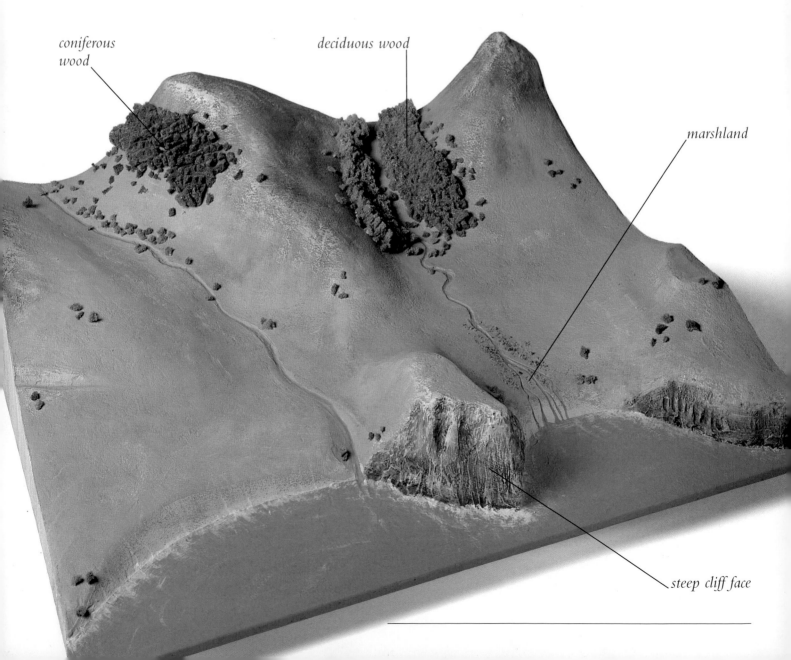

coniferous wood

deciduous wood

marshland

steep cliff face

△ *This photograph of a deciduous tree is simplified into a symbol of a tree with a bushy outline.*

△ *Coniferous trees are taller and more pointed so their symbol is a simple tree with four straight branches.*

How to design a symbol

A symbol needs to remind people instantly of the real feature it represents. Sometimes a symbol is a less complicated version of the real thing, such as the outline of a tree. Sometimes a symbol just shows the idea of the feature, such as a pair of trainers being used as a symbol for a sports center. It takes a lot of work to design a symbol that can be easily understood by a person looking at the map. When it is not possible to use a symbol, one or two large letters may be used instead, such as T for telephone.

∨ *This map uses symbols and colors to show the features of the landscape simply and clearly.*

Simple symbols

On a map, the symbols may be very small, so they work best if they are clear shapes with a few, bold lines. Solid shapes are easier to see than outlines when they are very small.

Unlocking maps

A **key** to a map explains what the symbols stand for. It contains the information needed to unlock the secrets of the map. Although it may be fairly obvious what some symbols represent, it is always worth checking the key to make sure you have understood the map correctly. A key is sometimes called a legend because it tells the story of the map.

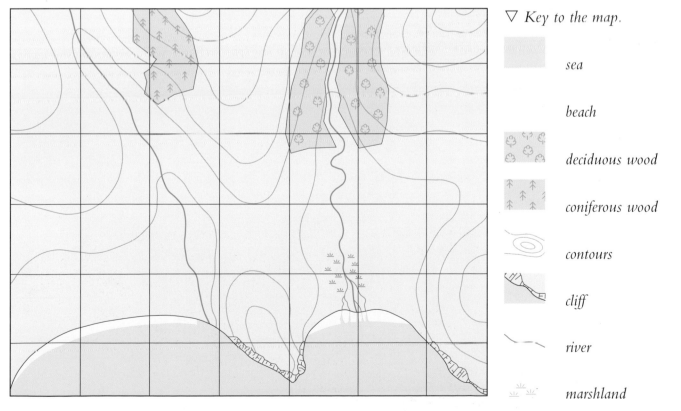

∇ *Key to the map.*

sea

beach

deciduous wood

coniferous wood

contours

cliff

river

marshland

Signs and symbols

🔦 👥 Building up the map

From roads and railroad tracks to towns and historical monuments, symbols for the human features of a landscape have to be added to a map. Maps show roads in different colors depending on their size. Interstate highways, for example, are usually colored red.

🔦 Symbols and scale

The size of a symbol and the amount of detail it can show depend on the type of map and the scale it is drawn to. For instance, a large city may be shown as only a square or a circle in an **atlas**. But on a large-scale map, the shape of the city can be clearly indicated.

👥 Maps and data

Sometimes, symbols may be used to represent data, or information, on maps. They may stand for numbers of things rather than actual features. For instance, a circle or a symbol of a person may stand for 1,000 people. A shipping map may use the thickness of lines to show how many ships travel from one port to another.

🔦 Separating the layers

At first glance, maps can appear rather complicated, like a very detailed painting. On the opposite page, we have peeled away the different layers that make up a map so you can see the different features to look out for.

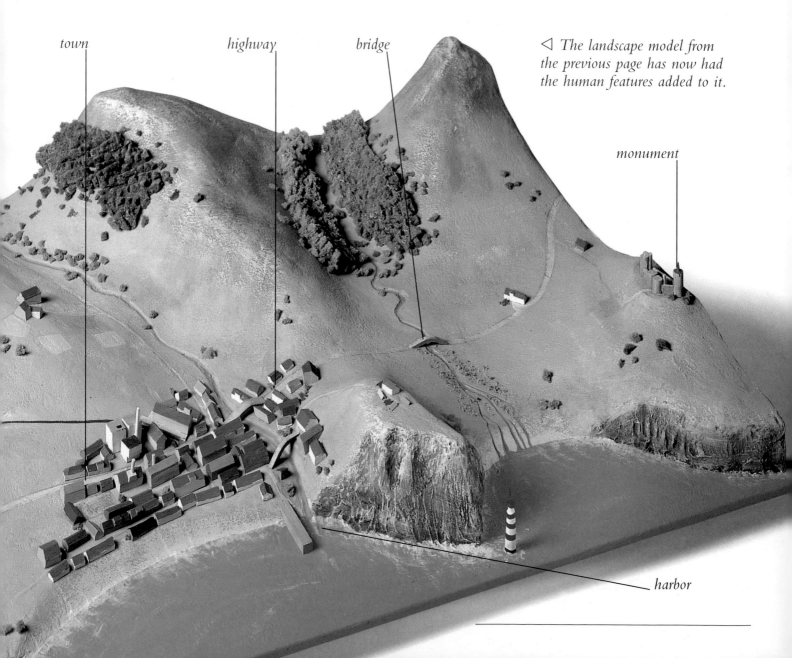

town   highway   bridge

◁ *The landscape model from the previous page has now had the human features added to it.*

monument

harbor

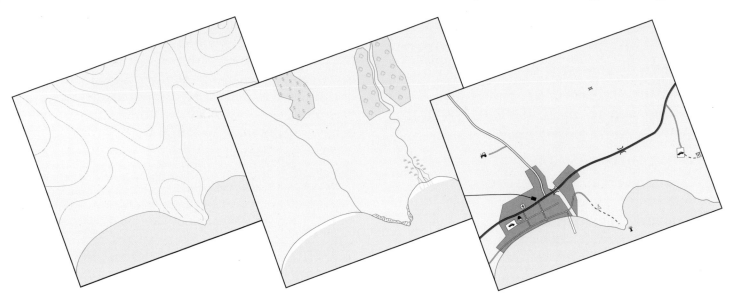

△ The contours show you the hills and valleys and the way the land slopes up and down.

△ Physical symbols show you natural features of the landscape, such as trees and rivers.

△ Human symbols show how people have changed the land by building towns, roads and farms.

▽ The final map shows all the layers placed on top of one another.

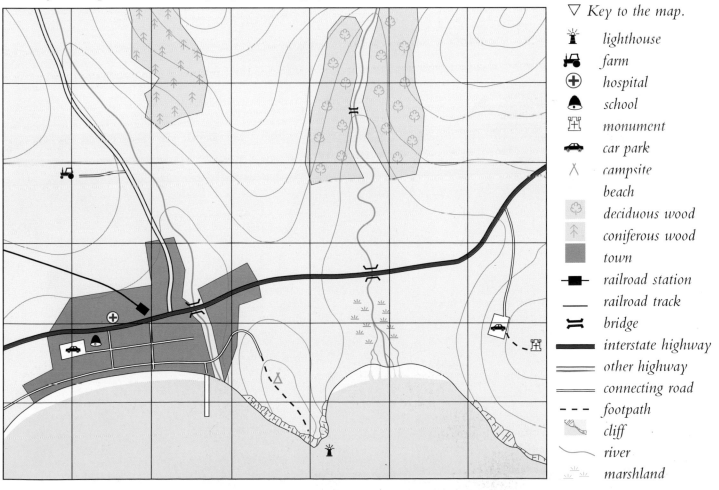

▽ Key to the map.

☀	lighthouse
🚜	farm
⊕	hospital
🔔	school
田	monument
🚗	car park
⋏	campsite
	beach
🌳	deciduous wood
🌲	coniferous wood
▮	town
■	railroad station
—	railroad track
⋈	bridge
▬	interstate highway
═	other highway
≡	connecting road
- - -	footpath
	cliff
	river
	marshland

Mapping the sea and sky

As well as mapping the landscape we can see, geographers also make maps of places we cannot see, such as under the ground, up in the sky or the deep-sea floor. These maps help people to plan buildings, make weather forecasts and search for fish, oil and minerals under the sea.

Tracking the weather

Satellites circling the Earth out in space give us an excellent view of how the weather is changing. They can spot a storm, such as a hurricane developing over the sea, and track its path to warn people of the danger that lies ahead. Information from satellites and weather stations on Earth is used to draw weather maps. Weather maps show the invisible movements of air that create the weather.

▷ *This map shows low pressure over the United Kingdom.*

High and low pressure

Lines called **isobars** join together places with the same air pressure—the weight of air pressing down on the Earth. The higher the number on the isobar, the higher the air pressure. High pressure usually brings dry weather, while lower pressure may bring rain or snow.

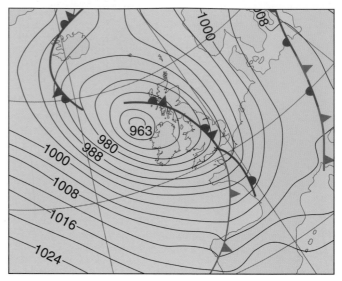

MAKE AN UNDERSEA MAP

You will need tank, wooden skewers, balsa wood, acrylic paints, tape, thick cardboard, bradawl, plasticine, waterproof pens

1 Cut a piece of cardboard slightly larger than the top of your tank. Draw a grid of $2/3$ in. squares on one side. Place the cardboard on top of the tank and use a skewer to poke holes through the center of each square.

2 Build a plasticine landscape on cardboard and decorate it with paint. Make a measuring stick by marking a skewer every $1/3$ in. from its point using a waterproof pen. Mark every fifth line in a different color.

3 Make a balsa-wood boat. Use a bradawl to make a hole through its center. Slide it onto the stick.

4 Position the landscape in the tank. Pour water into the tank as shown.

How do we map places we cannot see?

sound beams · sea floor

⛰ "Hearing" the sea floor

Satellites can't "see" through water, so maps of the sea floor have to be made using information collected in a different way. The sea's depth is measured using **sonar**, which stands for "*sound navigation and ranging.*" Sonar equipment sends beams of very high sounds called ultrasound down into the water. It then measures the time it takes for the echo of the sound to bounce back.

⛰ From beams to maps

We know how far sound travels in a certain time, so we can work out the distance from the surface of the sea to the sea floor. Information from sonar equipment, and from submarines that dive deep into the sea, has revealed that the sea floor has many mountains, volcanoes and valleys, just like dry land.

◁ *Echoes from the sound beams sent down by the ship tell us about the shape of the sea floor.*

5 Tape your grid on top of the tank. Starting in one corner, push the measuring stick through the cardboard until it touches the plasticine landscape, as shown at left. Now count the number of lines up to the surface of the water and write this number in the square in pencil. Do the same for every square.

6 To make your map of the sea floor, remove the cardboard from the tank and paint the squares. Areas of the same depth should be the same color. Try and use a gradual scale from white to dark blue, as shown below.

Human maps

People use land in all sorts of ways, from building roads and towns, to growing crops and raising farm animals. This information can be recorded on maps to help people find places and show how we change the landscape. These maps are called human maps.

—India

—Australia

△ *A population map of the world.*

👫 Plotting numbers

Sometimes it is useful to turn facts and figures into a map. In this way we can compare places and countries, and make predictions about the future. For example, maps can record population or the amount of energy people use. These are called **statistical maps**.

👫 Mapping population

On some world maps, such as the one above, the size of a country or continent relates to the size of its population, not to its real size. India is really smaller than Australia, but it is bigger on this map because more people live there. Compare this map to the world picture on page 5.

MAKE A STATISTICAL MAP

You will need simple local map, pens, pencils, ruler, colored paper, toothpicks, glue or tape, clipboard, watch

1 Ask an adult to take you to the middle of your town or village. Bring paper, a pencil and a watch with you.

2 For a traffic survey, stand at a crossroads and note down how many vehicles go down each road in five minutes. Do the same for several other crossroads in your area, as shown on the model opposite.

3 For a store survey, stand outside a store and count how many people visit it in five minutes. Do the same for other stores.

4 Indoors, plot your data on a local map. Use colored arrows to represent different numbers of vehicles in your traffic survey. For example, use a yellow arrow for fewer than 20 vehicles, an orange arrow for 20 to 40 vehicles, and so on. In a similar way, make flags of different heights for the different numbers of people visiting each store. Pin your symbols on the map.

▽ *Your final map shows which stores and roads are busiest.*

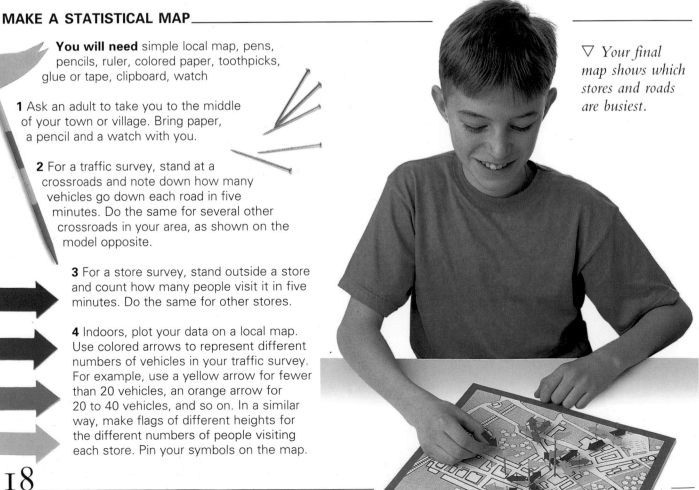

Coloring maps

Parts of a town or village are used in different ways. Some areas of land are used for farming, some for stores and offices, and others for places to live. **Land use maps** are colored to show where these different areas are.

People can use these maps to compare different places, such as town and countryside areas. They also help geographers understand how and why places change over time.

▽ *This model of a town shows where surveys were taken for the statistical map below left.*

MAKE A LAND USE MAP

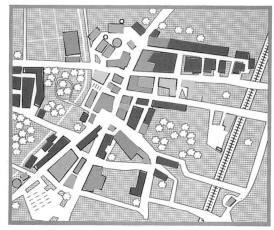

You will need local map, colored paper, pens, scissors, glue

1 Use a map of your town to help you draw a simple map of the area that you want to survey.

▽ *Key to the map.*

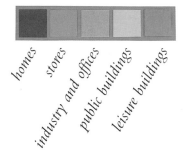

homes   stores   industry and offices   public buildings   leisure buildings

2 Find out what the different buildings are used for. Make a list of those which are used for stores, homes and so on.

3 Choose a different color for each type of land use. Then cut and glue colored paper shapes on each building to show how it is used. Finally, draw a key to explain your map.

yellow triangles show the crossroads where traffic surveys were made

blue triangles show where store surveys were made

Three-dimensional maps

People are used to seeing the shape of the land in three dimensions (3-D), so it isn't always easy to read a flat map and understand how the land looks. Some maps and **globes** are made with raised surfaces. These maps are used for teaching and also to help people who cannot see well or are blind. The disadvantage of 3-D maps is that they cannot be printed in books or folded up easily to fit in your pocket.

✏ 3-D symbols

Some flat maps, such as tourist maps or museum plans, include symbols drawn as if they are 3-D. They show buildings, rooms or other features drawn from the side, so they look more realistic. Some people feel this makes the maps easier to understand. But the symbols take up a lot of space and may hide other parts of the map.

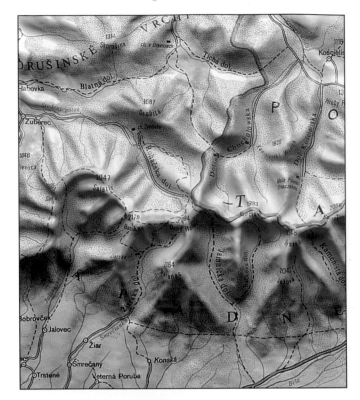

▽ *A 3-D map of the Tatra Mountains in Slovakia, eastern Europe.*

MAKE A 3-D MAP

You will need thick cardboard, tracing paper, tape, craft knife, glue, flour, newspaper, paints, paintbrush, maps

1 Find a map that shows several mountains, hills and other features such as rivers, villages or farms. Trace the contours onto tracing paper. You can enlarge a small part of the map on a photocopier to make the contours easier to trace.

2 Tape the tracing paper onto a piece of cardboard. Ask an adult to help cut around the lowest contour. Tape the remaining tracing paper onto another piece of cardboard and cut out the next contour. Repeat this for each contour in turn.

3 Glue the contour shapes in position on a cardboard base so the contours are in order of height, from the lowest to the highest. Contour lines on a map are like the edges of your layers of cardboard.

4 Cover the cardboard with layers of newspaper strips dipped in a flour and water paste. Leave to dry.

Computer images

On computer screens, it is possible to produce a 3-D picture of a landscape. These pictures can be moved around so they can be seen from different distances and different angles—from above, from the side, and so on. Now that people can look at the shape of the land so easily on screen, computers will be very useful in the future of mapmaking.

▷ *This is a 3-D computer image of mountains in Corsica, France. Vegetation is shown in red and the sea is dark blue. The sky was added by computer.*

▽ *Key to the map.*

harbor campsite town school telephone hospital farm coniferous wood

5 Paint the landscape and make symbols for the various features on the map. List your symbols in a key. Add an arrow pointing north (the grid lines on a map usually point upward to north).

Touch maps

People who cannot see well, or who are blind, can "read" maps with raised symbols and words that they feel with their fingertips. These special maps are called **tactual maps**.

▽ *This model was made from a map of the Cuillin Hills in Scotland.*

The globe

The Earth seems flat when you walk around on the surface, but you can see that it is round when you look at pictures taken from spacecraft. The only way to make an accurate map of the world is to build a globe, which shows the true positions of the land and sea. Globes can be made from 12 or more flat segments stuck onto a ball, or sphere. An imaginary line called the **equator** divides the northern half of the Earth from the southern half. Globes usually spin around and tilt at an angle like the Earth.

▽ *This satellite image of the Earth shows us that the world is not flat but round.*

BUILD A GLOBE

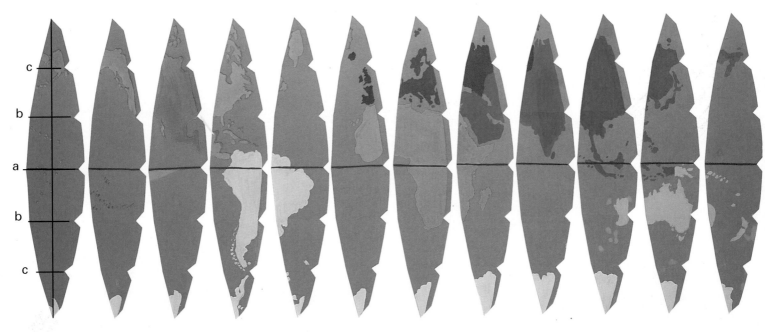

You will need glue, atlas, blue paper, cardboard, paints, dowel, plasticine

1 Draw a 16½ in. straight line on a piece of blue paper. Now draw five lines at right angles to this line to divide it into six equal sections. These lines—**a**, **b** and **c**—above, should be 2⅔ in., 2⅓ in., and 1½ in. long.

2 Join the end points of these lines together and add six tabs to make a segment, as shown above. Cut out the segment carefully. Cut 11 more segments the same size.

3 Draw the outlines of the continents on your segments. Use the model shown above as a guide.

4 Paint the land using appropriate colors. We have painted the seven continents in different colors. Paint the line of the equator in red, as shown above.

5 Fold each segment along the lines **a**, **b** and **c**, and glue the segments together as shown at right.

⊕ Which way round?

In space, there is no up and down or top and bottom, so you can view a globe with any part at the top. If you turn the globe so that the **South Pole** is at the top, you will get a very different view of the world.

⊕ Tilted Earth

Globes are usually tilted at an angle because the Earth leans slightly to one side, at an angle of 23.5 **degrees** from the sun. The tilt of the Earth means that some places receive different amounts of light and heat from the sun at different times of year. This produces weather changes that we call the **seasons**.

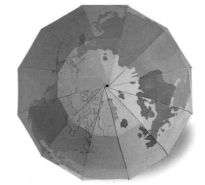

△ *Looking down on the Earth from the **North Pole**, you can see that many continents are clustered together at this end of the world.*

△ *One side of the Earth is nearly all blue—the Pacific Ocean. All the continents together would fit into an area the size of the Pacific Ocean.*

6 For the globe stand, make a cone with a piece of cardboard and push a large piece of plasticine inside. Push a piece of dowel through the globe and into the plasticine at an angle.

the equator

Dividing up the world

A grid of imaginary lines helps people to pinpoint different places in the world. The grid lines are called **longitude** and **latitude**. On a globe, lines of longitude meet at the poles, while lines of latitude run parallel to the equator. On a map, longitude lines go from top to bottom and latitude lines from side to side. Every place in the world can be located using longitude and latitude. For instance, New York is 40 degrees north (latitude) and 73 degrees west (longitude).

⊕ Where is north?

The true North Pole is right at the top of the world, in the middle of the Arctic Ocean. A **compass** needle, a tiny **magnet**, doesn't point to true north but to an area in northern Canada, called **magnetic north**. There is also a magnetic south pole. The magnetic poles move slightly from year to year.

magnetic north
true north
latitude lines
longitude lines

North Pole
line of latitude 30° north
the equator
30°

⊕ Latitude

The latitude of a place tells us its position north or south of the equator. The equator has a latitude of 0 degrees (0°). There are 90 "slices," or degrees, on each side of the equator, so the North Pole has a latitude of 90° north while the South Pole has a latitude of 90° south.

⊕ Moving north and south

Lines of latitude are measured in degrees because they are angles. Each line is the angle between two imaginary lines drawn from the center of the Earth to the surface. One line goes to the equator and the other to the line of latitude. This model shows the line of latitude 30° north.

MAKE A COMPASS

You will need magnet, needle, cork, plastic tub and lid, plasticine, bradawl, toothpick

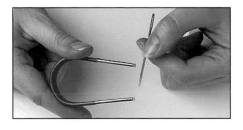

1 Place a large piece of plasticine in the tub and push a toothpick into the middle. Cut away most of the lid, leaving only the rim. Glue a ring of paper to the top side of the rim.

2 Use a bradawl to dig a hole ¹/₅ in. deep in the center of one end of the cork. Balance the cork on the end of the toothpick. Fill the tub with water until the cork floats. The toothpick stops the cork from floating to the side.

3 Make a needle into a magnet by stroking a real magnet toward the tip of the needle about 50 times.

4 Paint the tip of the needle and place it on the cork. The needle should now swing round to point north.

5 Put the rim in place. Mark north with a yellow triangle, as shown at right.

6 Place the compass on a local map and turn the map until the needle points to the top of the map. Your map now shows you the true direction of features in your area.

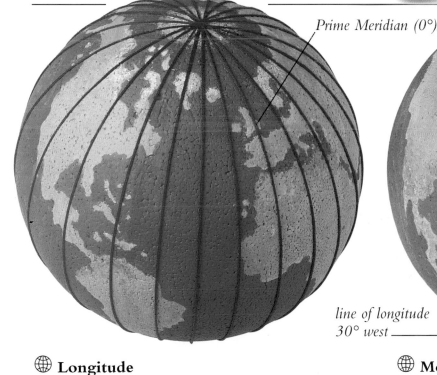

Prime Meridian (0°)

*line of longitude
30° west*

30°

🌐 Longitude
The longitude of a place tells us its position east or west of an imaginary line called the **Prime Meridian**. This line is drawn from the North Pole to the South Pole through Greenwich, in London, England. Lines of longitude divide the world up like segments of an orange.

🌐 Moving east and west
Lines of longitude are measured in degrees between two imaginary lines drawn from the center of the Earth to the equator. There are 180 degrees west and 180 degrees east of the Prime Meridian (0°). This model shows the line of longitude 30° west.

Mapping the globe

A drawing of the Earth's curved surface onto a flat surface is called a **map projection**. First the lines of latitude and longitude are drawn from a globe onto a sheet of paper. Then the continents and oceans are added. There are many different ways of projecting a globe onto a flat surface, but all of them distort the Earth in some way. Mapmakers have to choose carefully between projections, to find one that will best suit their purpose.

✎ ⊕ Stretching the world
No projection is ever as accurate as a globe map. It might distort the shape or size of the land, or show the wrong distances between continents. But projections do show parts of the world fairly accurately. There are three main kinds of projections: planar, conic and cylindrical. These are done by geographers using mathematics.

✎ ⊕ Planar projections
A planar projection makes a circular map and shows only half the world at a time. It is made as if one point on the globe is touching a flat surface and light is shone from the center of the globe. Most planar projections have the North or the South Pole in the middle, but the middle of the map can be anywhere on the globe.

MAKE MAP PROJECTIONS

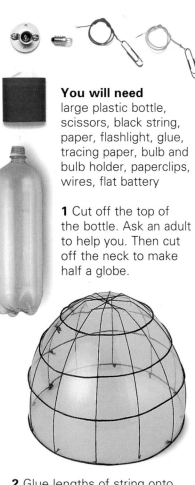

You will need
large plastic bottle, scissors, black string, paper, flashlight, glue, tracing paper, bulb and bulb holder, paperclips, wires, flat battery

1 Cut off the top of the bottle. Ask an adult to help you. Then cut off the neck to make half a globe.

2 Glue lengths of string onto the half globe to make lines of latitude and longitude.

3 For a planar projection, place your half globe on a piece of paper. Shine the flashlight into the middle of it, as shown. You will see the shadows of the latitude and longitude lines thrown out, or projected, onto the paper.

4 Connect the bulb to the battery using the wires and clips. Rest the bulb on the flat side of the battery.

5 For a conic projection, place the half globe upside down over the bulb and battery. Make a cone from tracing paper, so that it just fits over the half globe. The shadows show rings of latitude and straight lines of longitude.

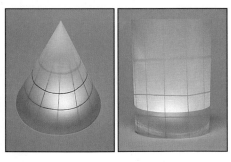

conic projection   *cylindrical projection*

6 For a cylindrical projection, fit a tube of tracing paper around the base of the half globe as shown above. The shadows produce horizontal lines of latitude and vertical lines of longitude.

Be careful! Don't let the tracing paper get too hot or it may burn. Ask an adult to help you.

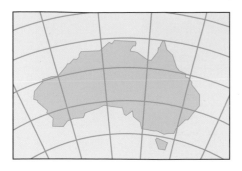

planar projection

conic projection

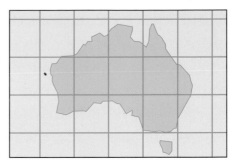

cylindrical projection

△ *These pictures of Australia show how various projections make maps look different. Map projections stretch the shape of a country in different ways.*

Conic projections

A conic projection creates a fan-shaped map. It is made as if light is shining through a globe onto a cone of paper wrapped around it. The most accurate part of the map is where the cone touches the globe. The map gets less accurate as you go farther from this line. It is useful for mapping countries in the middle of the globe, such as the United States.

Cylindrical projections

A cylindrical projection will give you a rectangular map. It is made as if a light shines through a globe onto a tube of paper wrapped around the globe. This projection can show almost the whole world, but it makes countries near the poles, such as Greenland, too big and stretched out. Countries farther from the poles, such as India, appear too small.

▽ *This cylindrical projection has been stretched and squashed so that areas are the right size but their shapes are distorted. Compare this map with a globe.*

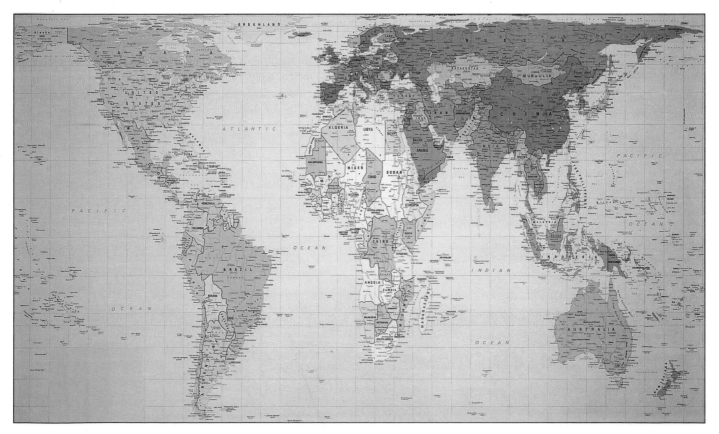

Early maps

People have been drawing maps for thousands of years. Over 4,000 years ago, people in Babylon (modern-day Iraq) drew maps on clay. Ancient Egyptians made maps from papyrus, a type of paper, and also developed ways of **surveying** the land.

△ *Inuit coastal maps were carved out of pieces of driftwood.*

📖 Building and carving maps

Over 500 years ago, people living in the Marshall Islands in the Pacific Ocean needed to be able to move between islands easily, for hunting and trading. They made maps out of sticks and shells. The sticks stood for the pattern of the ocean currents, and the shells marked the positions of islands. The Inuit, native people of Greenland and Canada, carved accurate wooden maps of the coastline. They used these maps to navigate on fishing and hunting trips.

△ *This Marshall Islands stick map was used to teach navigation as well as to plan journeys.*

📖 🌐 Maps of the world

The first world map was drawn by the Greek scholar Ptolemy in AD 160. At that time he did not know that America, Australia or Antarctica existed. During the Middle Ages—about AD 400 to the late 1400s—mapmaking progressed in China and the Arab world. The Chinese printed the first map in 1155, more than 300 years before maps were printed in Europe.

▷ *Compare this naval map of the Atlantic, drawn over 400 years ago by a mapmaker from Portugal, with a map in a modern atlas.*

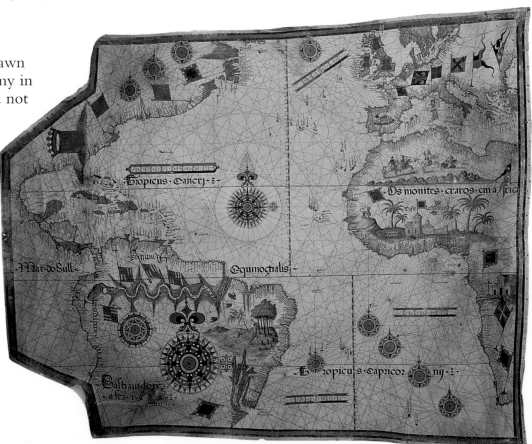

📓 Route maps

Religious pilgrims in the Middle Ages used strip maps with their routes across the country shown in straight lines. They read the maps from the bottom to the top of each column.

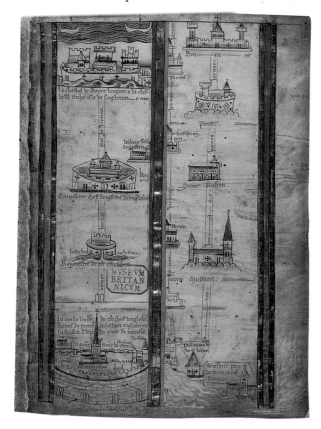

△ *This 13th-century route map shows the journey from London to Dover Castle, and then across the waves of the English Channel to two French towns.*

MAKE A ROUTE MAP

You will need paper, scissors, colored pens, cardboard

1 Write a list of the different stages of a journey you have been on recently, or of an imaginary journey. Make a note of interesting landmarks, such as towns and forests, and the time as you passed each one.

2 Draw a road going down the middle of a large piece of paper. Add clocks to show the start and finish times of the journey. On the map shown at right, lines are marked for every five minutes of the journey.

3 Starting at the bottom of the paper, add cardboard symbols for the different stages of your journey. Don't worry about drawing things to scale. The main point is to get all the different stages in the right order.

Surveying and measuring

To draw a map, mapmakers need to know about the shape of the land and the distance between points on the ground. People who gather this information are called land surveyors. Today, many of the measurements for maps come from pictures from satellites or **aerial photographs**, photographs taken from aircraft.

Angles and triangles

Many surveyors today still have to take measurements by walking across land. A good way to map a piece of land is to divide it into triangles. Surveyors use triangles because they can work out the lengths of the sides of a triangle by measuring mainly angles. This method is called **triangulation**. Surveyors use instruments called **theodolites** to measure angles between points of these triangles. A theodolite contains a small telescope and a level, and is mounted on a tripod.

Measuring with triangles

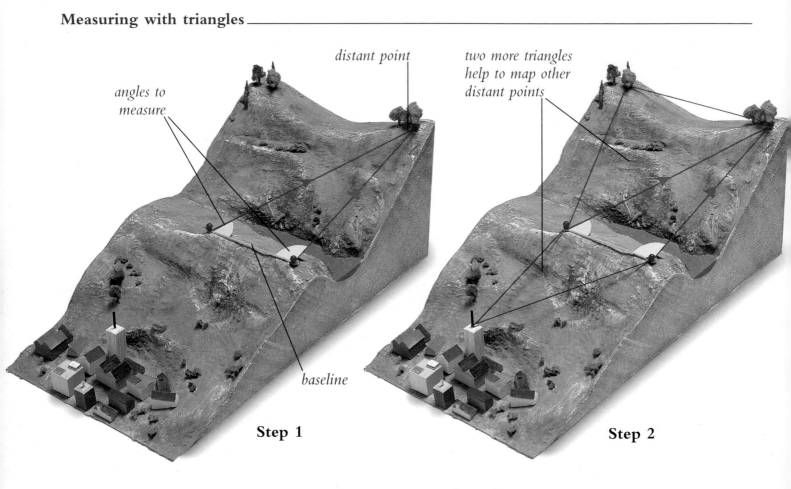

angles to measure

distant point

two more triangles help to map other distant points

baseline

Step 1

Step 2

1 Using a baseline

Surveyors first measure a short distance called a baseline. Standing at one end of the line, they measure the angle to a distant point—in this case, a tree. They then go to the other end of the baseline and measure the angle to the same point. Surveyors then use mathematics to work out the distances from the baseline to the tree.

2 Adding more triangles

The sides of this triangle are used as new baselines to work out other distances. Triangles are linked to the first, covering the whole area. This is useful because surveyors have to measure only one distance, the baseline, and from then on they measure only angles. In large areas, it is easier to measure angles than distances.

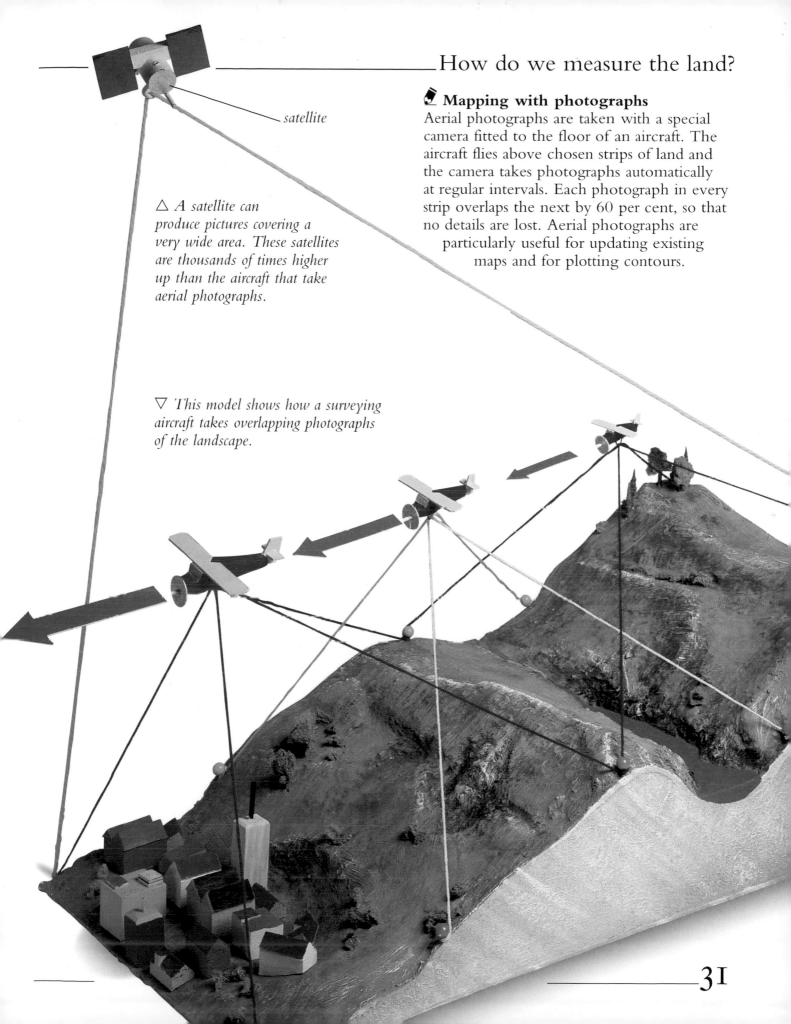

Mapping with photographs

Aerial photographs are taken with a special camera fitted to the floor of an aircraft. The aircraft flies above chosen strips of land and the camera takes photographs automatically at regular intervals. Each photograph in every strip overlaps the next by 60 per cent, so that no details are lost. Aerial photographs are particularly useful for updating existing maps and for plotting contours.

satellite

△ *A satellite can produce pictures covering a very wide area. These satellites are thousands of times higher up than the aircraft that take aerial photographs.*

▽ *This model shows how a surveying aircraft takes overlapping photographs of the landscape.*

Plotting maps

The art, science and technology of making maps is called cartography, and the people who draw maps are called cartographers. Having collected as much information as possible from surveyors, a cartographer has to decide what to include on the map and what to leave out. It is important to make sure the map is as clear and easy to read as possible.

🖊 Map drawing

The conventional way of drawing maps is called **scribing**. The cartographer carefully scrapes lines onto a film that is then used as a photographic stencil to print the layers of a map. Nowadays, instruments scan plans and aerial photographs, and turn them into information for drawing a map on a computer. Using a computer is much faster than scribing, and the maps can be easily updated if new information needs to be added.

△ *The hand control on this computer is used to scan maps so that they can be copied onto a screen.*

MAKE A 3-D VIEWER

You will need tracing paper, thin cardboard, thick cardboard, two small lenses, camera and tripod, tape, slide film

1 Load your camera with slide film. Then take a photograph of an object. Move the camera round slightly and take another photograph. You then need to have these pictures developed and made into slides.

2 Cut a cardboard shape like the one above. Each edge of the wide end of the viewer should measure 2 in. Cut a hole slightly smaller than your lens. Now fold and glue the cardboard to make the viewer. Glue a lens to the small end of the viewer.

▷ *Cartographers use very accurate images of the Earth which are produced by satellites in space.*

🌐 Curved Earth, flat maps

Small areas of the Earth are mapped as though the Earth is flat. But for large areas, mapmakers must allow for the fact that the surface of the Earth is curved. Mapmakers use mathematics to change the curved surface to a flat surface.

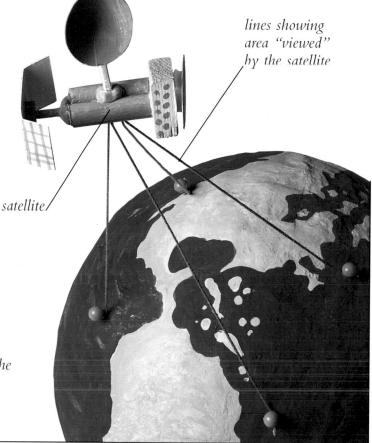

lines showing area "viewed" by the satellite

satellite

△ *This is a curved section of the Earth, as viewed by the satellite shown at right. Mapmakers correct distortions, especially in the corner areas, to make an accurate map.*

3 Cut thin cardboard and cardboard pieces as shown. They should be slightly larger than the slides. Tape tracing paper to the card window and glue the pieces on top of each other in the order shown.

4 Tape the slide holder to the wide end of the viewer with the rectangular window facing outward.

5 Now make another viewer in the same way. Place one of the slides in each viewer, and put a viewer to each eye. Hold the viewers close together and relax your eyes. You should see the pictures slide together. The object will pop up in 3-D. You may have to look at the object for some time before it works for you.

📷 Seeing in 3-D

When cartographers look at overlapping aerial photographs through a **stereoscope**, they see a 3-D picture of the land—even though the photographs are flat. They see the view as if they were looking down from the plane that took the photograph. Seeing in 3-D helps them to pick out features and show how the land goes up and down.

📷 How stereoscopes work

When we look at an object, each eye sees a slightly different view. Our brain combines these views to make a 3-D image. In the same way, a stereoscope combines the two views so that we see the picture in 3-D.

Making your own map

Over the next six pages, you will find out how to survey and map a small local area, such as a park. This will help you to understand the different stages involved in making maps. After making your measuring tools, turn to pages 36-37 to learn how to use them outdoors to survey a piece of land. Finally, look at pages 38-39 to learn how to draw your map to scale.

Types of tools

Surveyors measure distances with instruments that use lasers or sound waves. These tools are very accurate and make it easy to measure distances over rough ground. You can measure distances with a trundle wheel that clicks every yard as it rolls. Theodolites are complicated tools for measuring angles. You can measure angles more easily using a bearing board, a tube that moves around on a board with degrees marked on it.

MAKE A TRUNDLE WHEEL

You will need thick cardboard, glue, length of $1/5$ in. dowel, two corks, drill, strips of wood, paints, nail, hammer, tape, bradawl, thin cardboard, drawing compass

3 Make holes through the corks with a bradawl. Push the dowel through one of them, as shown above.

1 Cut three long strips of wood and one short strip, as shown above. Drill a $1/5$ in. hole at the end of two long pieces. Glue the pieces together to make a fork shape. The holes should be at the ends of the fork prongs. Cut four thin cardboard circles. Each circle should be 6 in. from the center to the outside.

2 Glue the circles of thin cardboard together to make the wheel. Divide each side into quarters and paint them in two colors as shown below.

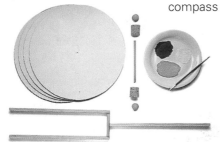

4 Make a hole through the middle of the wheel and push the dowel through. Slide the other cork onto the other side of the dowel. Glue the corks to the wheel and dowel. Now stick a folded piece of thin cardboard near the edge of the wheel as shown. Tape around the edge of the wheel.

5 Hammer a nail into the inside of one fork prong about $5^1/_2$ in. above the hole. Slip the wheel into the fork. As the wheel turns, the nail should click against the cardboard. Wind tape around the wood for a handle.

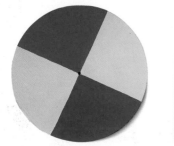

MAKE A BEARING BOARD

You will need thick cardboard, paper fastener, colored paper, protractor, magnetic compass, drawing compass, scissors, glue, tape, broom handle

1 Cut out a 12 in. square of thick cardboard and a square of colored paper the same size. Glue the cardboard and paper together to make the base of your bearing board.

2 Using a drawing compass, draw a ring of different colored paper slightly smaller than the base. Cut it out and glue it to the base.

3 Use a protractor to divide the colored ring into 360°. Label every 10° on the yellow ring and write the number next to each line. Glue a magnetic compass into the board with the north arrow pointing to 0°/360°.

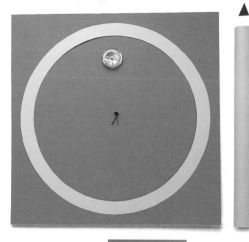

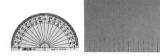

Now turn the page to see how to use your tools to make a map.

pointer

compass

4 Roll up a sheet of colored paper and tape the edges to make a tube 12 in. long. Cut a small triangle pointer in a different color and glue this in one end of the tube.

5 Make a hole in the center of your board and push a paper fastener through it. Cut a small slit about a third of the way along the tube. Slip the round head of the fastener through the slit. Make sure the tube can turn right round the circle.

6 Now cut a small piece of cardboard to fit around the broom handle. Cut slits into the top of the cardboard, then roll it up into a tube and glue it onto the broom handle, making sure the cut end sticks up above it. Press the slits outward to make a flat surface. Glue to the underside of the bearing board.

Making your own map

✎ Taking measurements

Once you have made your measuring tools, the next step is to choose a small area to map. An area of about 8,000 square feet is a good size. Make sure the area has several fixed features such as paths, trees, a slide or a pond. A fairly open area is best so you don't get confused between features. To work out where to plot the features on your map, you will need to measure angles and distances to each feature.

✎ Planning your survey

Surveyors need to choose a suitable base point from which to take measurements. Find a position roughly in the middle of your area that has a clear view of most of the main features. You need to choose a place you can easily find again. If you don't finish all your measurements, you may need to return there another day.

Make a sketch of the area including all the features you want to plot on your map. Draw lines to each feature from your base point, as on the model below. Distances are not important at this stage. You are now ready to take your measurements. Use a magnetic compass to mark a north arrow on your sketch.

distances to measure

take measurements from this base point

◁ A small park like this one is a good area in which to practice your mapping skills.

MEASURE ANGLES

1 Start at the base point. Hold the bearing board you made on page 35 in a level position. Looking at the compass, turn the board until 0° is pointing north.

2 Look through the tube at the feature you want to plot on your map. The arrow at the end of the tube will be pointing at one of the angles around the edge of the board.

3 Write down the angle next to the feature on your sketch map. Do the same for each of the features in your area.

MEASURE DISTANCES

1 Start at the base point. Hold the trundle wheel you made on page 34 upright so the nail sits behind the folded piece of cardboard, as shown below.

2 Push the trundle wheel in a straight line from the base point to the first feature. Count how many times it clicks. The wheel you have made clicks every yard. So if the wheel clicks five times, it has measured 5 yds.

3 Write down the distance to each feature next to the distance lines on your sketch map.

Turn to pages 38-39 to see how to use these measurements to plot a map.

Making your own map

📝 Plotting your measurements

To plot an accurate map of your area, you will use all the measurements that you marked on your sketch map. You need to decide on a scale for your map, as explained below. The map should include as much information as possible, but still be clear and easy to read. Choose colors that stand out well.

📝 Showing height

You can also show where the land goes up and down by using shading or a color code for high and low ground. Look carefully at a local map of your area and read the contours to work out how high the land is above sea level.

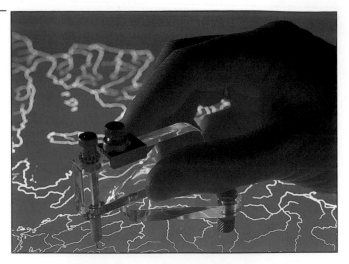

△ *This cartographer uses a sapphire-tipped scriber to scrape fine lines in film when plotting a map by hand.*

DRAW YOUR OWN MAP

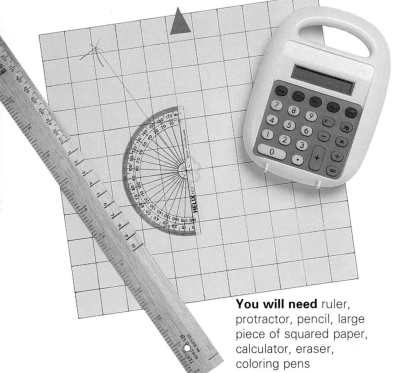

You will need ruler, protractor, pencil, large piece of squared paper, calculator, eraser, coloring pens

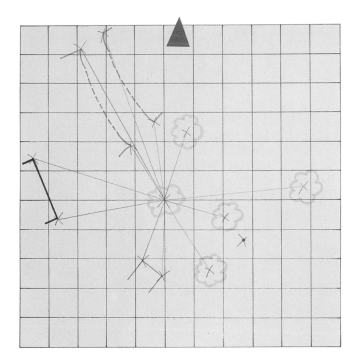

1 To find the scale for your map, first divide the size of the area you are mapping by the size of your paper. For instance, if your area is 100 ft. along one side and your paper is 10 in., you need to divide 100 ft. by 10 in.

2 You can't divide the two numbers because one is measured in feet and the other in inches. But by knowing that there are 12 in. in 1 ft., you can work out that 100 ft. is the same as 1,200 in. You are now able to do the sum. 1,200 in. divided by 10 in. is 120, so the scale is 1:120. This means that 1 in. on the map equals 120 in. (10 ft.) on land.

3 With a calculator, work out your own scale and change the distances on your sketch map to this scale. In the center of your paper, mark the base point with its symbol. Mark the direction of north with an arrow. North is at 0°.

4 With a protractor, plot the angle of the first feature from the base point. The angle marked above left is 330°. Draw a line of correct length in the direction of this angle.

5 At the end of each line, put a small dot or cross. Then draw in a colored symbol for each feature in the correct position. For larger features, you will need to draw two or more lines to fix their positions accurately.

⊗ Making a grid

You could use the lines on squared paper to make a grid. Write numbers between the grid lines along one edge of the map and letters along the other edge. If you wanted to meet a friend at a point on the map, you could give them a grid reference for how to get there.

◪ A record of the past

Maps are a useful record of the history of a place. If new roads, houses, paths or other features are built, they must be added to a map of the area. Every month, update a map of your area to see the changes that take place over a whole year.

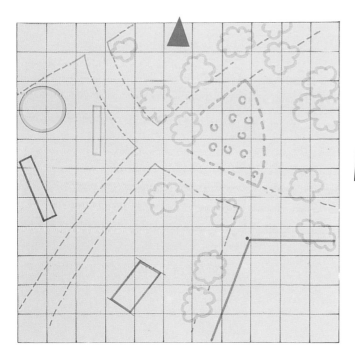

6 Erase the pencil lines from the base point to each feature. You could also add a border to the map or any colored shading in the background that makes the map easier to read. For instance, you could color the water in a pond. Finally, draw a key at the side of the map to explain the symbols and colors you have used.

You could also plot your map on a computer. This is useful as the map can be updated if the area changes. New features can be added or old features taken away. Names can be changed easily. Several copies of the map can also be printed out and the map scale changed without drawing the map all over again.

▽ *This map was drawn on a computer. Some computer programs for drawing simple maps have small symbols like these already prepared for you to position.*

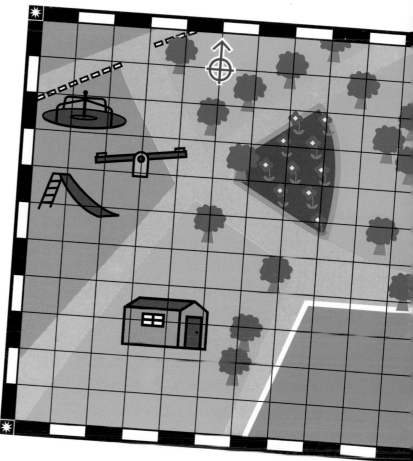

∨ *Key for the map shown above.*

slide

merry-go-round

see-saw

shed

tree

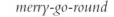
fence

water

flower bed

Finding your way

Maps help you find your way to places, especially if you have never been there before. To prepare for a journey, it is a good idea to work out the best route on a map. Most cities have street maps showing the roads, important buildings and park areas in detail. You can use the scale of a map to measure the distance of your journey.

△ *This aerial photograph shows the grid pattern of the streets in New York City.*

✦ Maps and settlements

Some modern cities, such as New York and Los Angeles, are built in a series of squares. This grid pattern makes it easier for people to find their way around. The roads have numbers and directions, such as north, south, east and west—East 64th Street, for example. Older cities often have more winding streets, especially in the center, which sometimes make places more difficult to find.

USING A STREET MAP

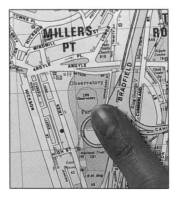

1 The first step is to look in the index. This gives you the grid reference for the right square on the map. For instance, the Observatory in Sydney, Australia, is in square D4.

2 Find the letter on the sides of the map and the number on the bottom or top of the map. You can now follow the lines into the map until your fingers meet.

3 This is the square you want. Look carefully within the square to find the road or feature you need. Use the same steps to find out where you are on the map at the moment.

4 Figure out the best way to get to your destination. If you look at the scale on the map, you can calculate how far you have to travel. Then you can decide on the best way to get there.

⚥ Other route maps

Some maps are not drawn to scale. If they were they would be too confusing. On subway maps, the systems of lines and stations are spread out neatly and drawn in straight lines so it is easy to find a station and plan a route. The distances between stations are not accurate. Sometimes bus-route maps and road maps are also drawn like this to make them easier to read.

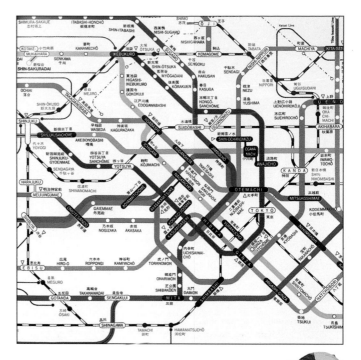

▷ *This map of the Tokyo subway system is not drawn to scale. Each route is a different color to make the lines easier to follow.*

⚥ How far is your journey?

To measure distances on a map, you may be able to use a ruler. For curved routes, you need a piece of string or wool, the edge of a piece of paper, or a special mini-trundle wheel.

MAKE A MINI-TRUNDLE WHEEL

You will need cardboard, pin, maps, paint, drawing compass, strip of wood

1 Draw two circles on the cardboard. To make a wheel for a 1:25,000 scale map, the radius of the circle should be 1 in. For a 1:50,000 scale map, make the radius 1/2 in. This will give you a wheel that turns once every 2 1/2 mi. on your map. Or you can draw any size circle and simply roll the finished wheel along the linear scale (see page 8) to see how far it measures in one turn.

2 Divide the circles into quarters and paint them as shown. Glue them together. Mark a start line on the edge between two quarters.

3 Now pin the wheel through its center to a short wooden strip as shown, so that the wheel moves round freely.

4 To use the wheel, line up the start line with the upper edge of the handle and roll it along your chosen route. Count the number of turns the wheel makes

5 To work out the distance, multiply the number of turns by the distance covered in one turn. If your wheel turns once every 2 1/2 mi. on the map and your wheel turns five times, the total distance of the route is 12 1/2 mi.

Finding your way

⚸ Plotting a route

The map below is being used to plan a walking route. The colored figures show sights to visit. The orange figures mark a castle and a beach, sights to visit on a short walk from the campsite. The red figures show sights for a longer river valley walk that includes a view from a hill. It is best to work out the distance of a walk before you start so you know how long it might take. You can cover 2-3 miles in an hour. Knowing how to use a compass will help to keep you on the right track.

▽ *Look at this map and think about routes you might take on a walk from the campsite.*

HOW TO USE A COMPASS

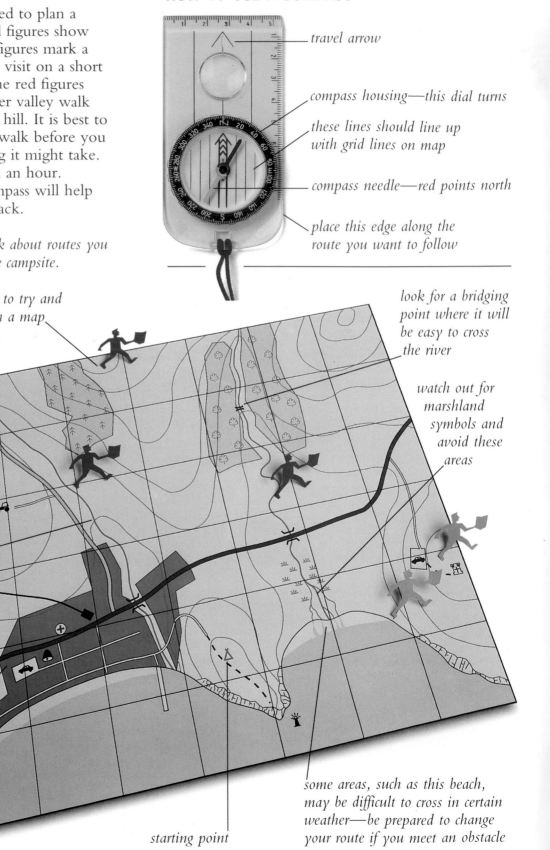

travel arrow

compass housing—this dial turns

these lines should line up with grid lines on map

compass needle—red points north

place this edge along the route you want to follow

the top of a hill is a good spot to try and identify the features marked on a map

look for a bridging point where it will be easy to cross the river

watch out for marshland symbols and avoid these areas

the bottom of a river valley is usually flat, which makes walking easier

it can be difficult finding your way out of a town as buildings often block your view

starting point

some areas, such as this beach, may be difficult to cross in certain weather—be prepared to change your route if you meet an obstacle

How do you plan a walking route?

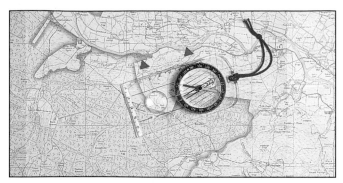

1 Place the straight edge of the compass on the map so that the travel arrow points along the route you want to follow.

2 Turn the compass housing so the lines in the circle line up with the grid lines on the map. The red arrow points to the top of the map. Ignore the compass needle for now.

3 Hold the compass and map horizontal, at about waist height, and turn yourself around until the compass needle swings above the red arrow in the circle. This is the north/south line.

4 Holding the map and compass, move off following the direction of the travel arrow on the edge of the compass—not the direction of the compass needle.

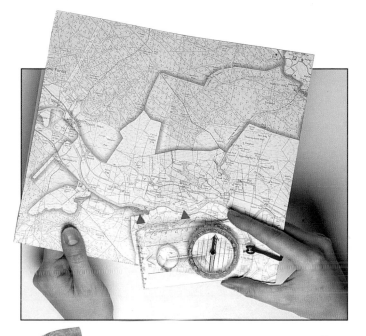

red route

yellow route

⊗ The chosen routes

The yellow route marked on this model follows a road or path where possible and avoids steep hills. Most of the red route is across rough countryside and there are some steep climbs. Think of other routes you could take.

⊗ Before you go

If you set out on a long walk, remember to take your map and compass with you. Take warm and waterproof clothing, food and drink. Always go with an adult.

◁ *This model shows two routes: the yellow route is easier, the red route is more challenging.*

Changing maps

People will always need new maps because the world is changing all the time. New roads, towns and airports, as well as natural changes to the surface of the Earth, must be recorded. Satellite images are becoming more useful to mapmakers for updating maps, as well as for making new types of maps. Satellite images of other planets are now being used to map surfaces people have never even walked on.

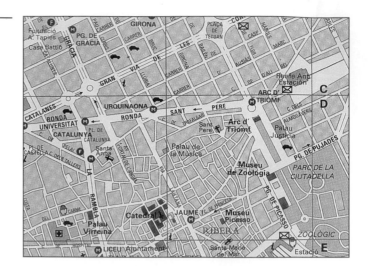

△ On this map of Barcelona in Spain, the straight lines of the newer streets fill the space around the shorter, denser streets of the old city.

🏔 Birth of an island

Sometimes new pieces of land, such as volcanic islands, appear on the Earth. When a volcano erupts under the seabed, the hot lava cools to form land that may rise above the surface of the water. The resulting island now has to be added to a map so that sea travelers can plan their routes accurately.

▷ This model shows the three stages of a volcanic eruption that produce a new island.

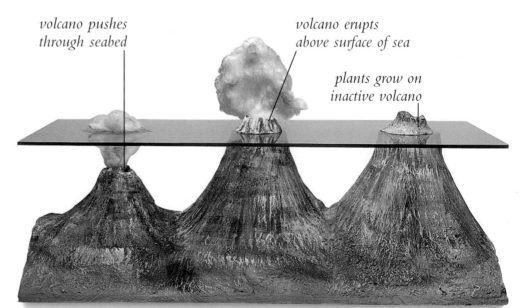

volcano pushes through seabed

volcano erupts above surface of sea

plants grow on inactive volcano

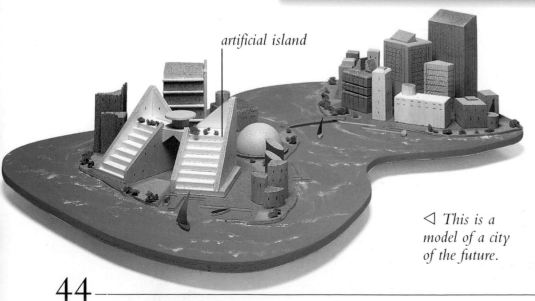

artificial island

◁ This is a model of a city of the future.

👫 Artificial land

In places where there is not much land for building, such as Hong Kong or Japan, people plan to build artificial islands. Airports may be built on these islands so that the noise of the aircraft is farther from places where people live. Whole cities may even be built on artificial land one day. Maps will have to record these new pieces of land and the buildings on them.

⊕ Satellite sensors

Satellite technology is advancing all the time. As well as being able to "see" smaller pieces of land, satellites now have special sensors to detect different types of land. These satellite pictures are usually taken with special infrared film that shows vegetation in red and roads and buildings in blue. Nowadays, satellites can even tell us where to drill for oil.

▷ *This picture of Tokyo, Japan, was taken with infrared film. Plants are red and buildings are blue so mapmakers can clearly see the types of land use.*

✎ New kinds of maps

In the future, computers will be used more often to record data for maps and to draw maps. Advances in technology have already led to "talking" maps in cars. These computer maps show drivers the best routes, avoiding traffic jams and road construction. Instead of paper maps, electronic maps of the future could appear on a pocket TV screen at the touch of a button.

▽ *This is a computer-generated map of one side of the moon. It shows the different types of minerals that make up the moon's surface.*

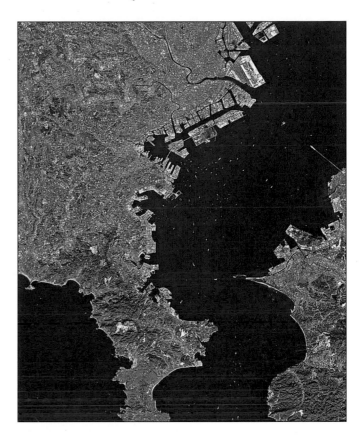

⊕ Mapping space

Maps are not limited to features here on Earth. Satellites and other spacecraft have sent back information that enables us to map distant stars and the surfaces of planets. These maps help scientists to understand the universe and investigate the geography of other worlds.

blue areas show a mineral found in low land

this part of the moon shows its natural color

red areas show a mineral found in high land

Glossary

aerial photograph A picture taken from the sky, usually from an airplane. Aerial photographs may be taken from directly overhead, or at an angle.

atlas A book of maps.

bench mark A mark cut in rocks, posts or buildings to mark the height of the land above sea level.

cartography The science and art of mapmaking. A cartographer is someone who draws maps.

compass A magnetic compass is an instrument used to find directions. It has a needle that points to magnetic north.

continent One of the big land masses of the world. There are seven continents: Africa, Europe, North America, South America, Asia, Australia and Antarctica.

contour A line on a map that joins places of the same height above sea level.

degree A unit for measuring angles. Lines of latitude and longitude are measured in degrees. The symbol for degrees is °. For example, 30 degrees is written 30°.

equator An imaginary line around the middle of the Earth, that divides the Earth into two equal halves—the northern hemisphere and the southern hemisphere.

global Relating to the whole world.

globe A sphere that shows the true positions of the land and sea areas on the Earth. A globe is usually tilted at an angle and spins around just like the Earth.

grid A series of equally spaced vertical and horizontal lines drawn on a map. A grid reference tells people which rows and columns to follow to find any point quickly and easily.

hachures Short black lines used to show very steep slopes on maps. They are often used to represent steep cliffs on maps.

human map A map showing information about how people use the land for homes, travel, shopping, farming and so on.

isobar A line on a weather map that joins points of equal air pressure.

key A list explaining all the symbols on a map. It is sometimes called a legend.

land use map A map that shows, usually in the form of a color code, how people use the land.

latitude Imaginary lines that run horizontally around the world parallel to the equator. They are sometimes called parallels.

longitude Imaginary lines that run at right angles to the equator and meet at the North and South Poles. They are also called meridians.

magnet A material that produces a magnetic force that attracts some metals, such as iron. The Earth behaves like a giant magnet because of the dense core of iron in its center.

magnetic north The point to which the needle on a compass points. The magnetic north pole is near the true North Pole of the Earth, but its position slowly changes over the years.

map projection A way of showing the surface of the Earth as a flat map. There are three main types of projection: planar, conic and cylindrical.

North Pole The northern end of the Earth's axis. It lies within the Arctic Circle. The North Pole is sometimes called true north.

physical map A map showing features of the Earth, such as rivers and rocks.

plan An outline drawing of an object or a place as seen from above. A plan usually shows a smaller area than a map.

Prime Meridian The line of 0° longitude that passes from the North Pole to the South Pole through Greenwich, in London, England.

rain forest Areas of dense forest near the equator where it is hot and wet all year round.

satellite An unmanned spacecraft placed in orbit around the Earth or another planet. Pictures taken from satellites are a vital source of information to mapmakers.

scale The number of units on the ground shown by one unit on a map. On a 1:120 map, 1 in. represents 120 in. (10 ft.) on the ground.

scribing A method used to scrape the lines needed on a map onto a piece of plastic film.

seasons Changes in the weather throughout the year. Some places have four seasons— spring, summer, autumn and winter. Others have wet and dry seasons. Seasons are caused by the Earth leaning at an angle as it moves around the sun.

sonar A way of using very high sounds, called ultrasounds, to measure distances and pinpoint the position of objects.

South Pole The southern end of the Earth's axis, It lies in the continent of Antarctica.

spot height The exact height of a point marked on a map.

statistical map A way of showing numbers in the form of a map. Statistical maps can be used to compare towns or countries.

stereoscope A device used to view aerial photographs so they appear in three dimensions.

surveying Measuring distances and angles to determine the size, shape, position and height of the land. The person who carries out this work is called a surveyor.

symbol A small picture or special shape on a map that stands for a real feature.

tactual map A map with raised symbols that blind people can read by touch.

theodolite An instrument used by surveyors to measure angles.

three-dimensional (3-D) Something having height as well as length and width. A flat map has only two dimensions.

triangulation A method used for surveying the land by measuring a series of triangles.

valley A long, low area mainly enclosed by hills. A valley often has a river running along it.

Index

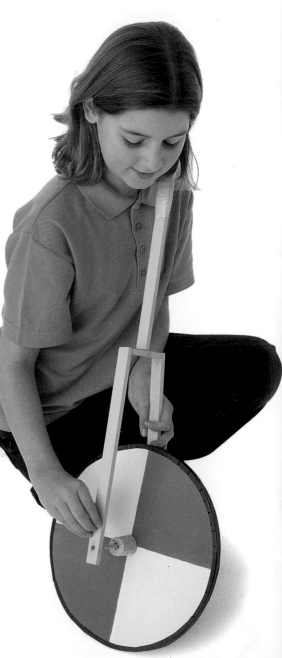